WASHINGTON D.C.

WASHINGTON D.C.

CRESCENT

AMERICA'S Federal capital, Washington, D.C., is undoubtedly among the more pleasant of the world's capital cities: broad, tree-lined streets and avenues, plenty of parks and open spaces, not too many dominant and insistent giant office blocks to spoil the proportions of the dignified Classical-style public buildings, and an on-the-whole placid, friendly front presented to the world.

It is also unique among the great cities of the world: a seat of government, a large city with a growing population, and a symbol of national pride all at the same time, it was the first national capital to be consciously planned as such. Perhaps to men who had just framed a Constitution that would shape the future of a whole nation, the deliberate planning of a capital city seemed nothing extraordinary, but it was not until well into the twentieth century that other nations were willing to assume the same tremendous challenge.

The United States Congress decided in July 1790, that the new seat of government should be situated on the Potomac River, between the states of Maryland and Virginia – a compromise area, in fact, between the states of the North and of the South. Hitherto, Congress had met at Philadelphia, among other towns. Other states were vying for the privilege of housing the nation's capital, and it was hoped that an entirely new town in its own federal enclave would resolve the squabbling. The city would be called Washington, in honor of the nation's first President and the district which encompassed it would be named Columbia, after Christopher Columbus.

The state of Maryland contributed 69 square miles of its territory to form the District of Columbia, and the state of Virginia nearly 31 square miles. Thus Washington, D.C. came into being: a fairly flat area of orchards, tobacco fields, plantations and swamp set on the banks of a river which took its name from the Indian word for 'trading place' – potomack.

George Washington is said to have been modestly embarrassed that the new capital was being named after him. He was, however, not so embarrassed that he would not give the city the best possible chance to succeed. He commissioned a

Gilbert Stuart, an American artist, painted several portraits of George Washington. The painting above was completed in 1795 and is known as the Vaughan portrait.
One of fifty placed at the base of the Washington Monument, the star-spangled banner left represents a State of America.

brilliant French army engineer, Major Pierre Charles L'Enfant, who had fought on the side of the colonies in the War of Independence, to draw up a plan for the new city. Although L'Enfant was relieved of the commission after a year because he refused to hurry the job and it was also proving to be very expensive, it is his basic plan which has given Washington its present-day layout.

In the 1790s, the plan seemed grandiose in the extreme for what was then and was to remain for decades a small town in the eyes of the world. "Few people would live in Washington, I take it, who were not obliged to live there…" reported Charles Dickens in 1842. Major L'Enfant drew up a plan for a city based on a grid system. The resulting blocks were broken by diagonal streets and avenues of splendid width, with squares and circles,

or *rond-points,* at intervals to add interest. The open vistas along the great avenues would be splendid, indeed, as befitted the capital of a great nation.

In any event, the city planners have been proved right. Washington has grown even to surpass the original grand conception and L'Enfant's plans, redis-covered in the 1880s, have provided the impetus for much of the twentieth-century town planning in Washington.

The grid system is basic to Washington's street layout. The streets running east and west of the Capitol Building have been numbered: 1st, 2nd, 3rd, 4th, etc., and those running north and south have been given letters: A Street, B Street, C Street etc. The avenues cutting diagonally across the grid are named after States: Pennsylvania, Massachusetts, New Jersey, Colorado.

The city has been further divided into four recognized areas, or quadrants, with Capitol Hill at its center. Lines drawn north and south, east and west through the Capitol split the city into the northwest (NW), northeast (NE), south-west (SW) and southeast (SE) quadrants, and these designations are essential parts of all city addresses. The northeast and southeast quadrants are largely residential areas; the southwest quadrant has seen the largest amount of urban renewal and slum clearance in the city; and the northwest quadrant is where most things happen, for this area contains many of the monuments and buildings which attract visitors to Washington, most of the hotels, and the best shops and restaurants.

In one respect the city does not conform to the original plans; it is considerably smaller. In 1846, the state of Virginia asked to have returned to it, and was granted, its original contribution to the federal capital, which included the town of Alexandria, where Washington had lived, and Arlington County.

Today, the District of Columbia has a total area of just over 69 square miles (the original contribution from the state of Maryland); but, take away the area covered by the Potomac and Anacostia Rivers, and there remains just 60.1 square miles of land, nearly a fifth of which is devoted to parks and recreation grounds.

INTRODUCTION

Within this relatively small area lies one of the most influential cities in the world; a splendid array of marble monuments, buildings whose outlines are recognized the world over, vast governmental offices, tree-lined streets, attractive parks and – a matter of concern for city planners who have been doing much to erase the shame of past indifference – areas of slum, all of which add up to home for nearly a million people.

To outsiders, most of these people may seem to be part of a city which has only one purpose – government. It is true that Washington has almost no other major industry, and the hopes of its original planners, including L'Enfant, that Washington would become the home of a great national university have not been realized.

Washington has several universities, including George Washington University, Georgetown University, Catholic University and Howard University, the latter founded in 1867 to provide for the educational needs of the newly-freed slaves, but the United States' greatest seats of learning are found elsewhere. In the John F. Kennedy Center for the Performing Arts, opened in 1971, Washington has a superbly designed series of concert halls and exhibition areas, but it seems unlikely that the Center will become a jumping-off point for new ideas in art, music or drama.

But, in fact, many of Washington's residents are not engaged in government but rather in the service industries, for the city does have a major 'hidden industry' – tourism. Nearly twenty million visitors now come to Washington every year from all over the world as well as from every state in the nation.

Many Americans come because they have business with their congressmen, the government, or one of its many federal agencies. Far more, however, come because Washington is a national symbol; here the history of the United States takes on an awesome reality and a sense of unchanging permanence. Most Americans and, indeed, most foreigners, are reduced to a reverent silence when confronted with the original Constitution document enshrined in its theft-proof, nuclear-

bomb-proof gold case in the National Archives, or with Daniel Chester French's deeply impressive statue of Abraham Lincoln seated in his marble shrine on the banks of the Potomac.

Much of the city that the tourists visit has come into being only in the twentieth century. The nineteenth century was, on the whole, not a time for careful town planning in Washington, particularly in the Civil War period when Washington became an armed camp overlooked by a

Capitol Building with an unfinished dome and an uncompleted Washington Monument. The 1870s saw a big – and very expensive – cleaning-up operation supervised by "Boss" Shepherd, chief of Public Works. Paved streets and sidewalks were laid down, and gas lighting installed along them; water mains and sewage systems were built, and thousands of trees planted.

Seen from the end of the Mall is the impressive Capitol Building top left, *while the skyline of the city is dominated by the Washington Monument* bottom left *at 555 feet. Commanding views of the city and parts of Maryland and Virginia may be seen from the top of the Monument.*
The National Gallery of Art center left and right *houses many famous paintings, including one of Raphael's early masterpieces "Small Cowper Madonna"* above, *painted in 1504.*

INTRODUCTION

The city's centennial in 1900 was another opportunity for a good look at how the nation's capital was faring, and it was in the years leading up to World War I that present-day Washington really began to take shape. Beautiful white marble, which is now such a feature of the city, began to appear and when the National Gallery of Art was opened in 1941 it was the largest marble building in the world. Green parks and trees grew and the mile-long Mall and the Federal Triangle were planned, though not to be completed for a couple of decades. In 1912 Washington received its most delicate touch of decoration when the famous cherry trees were planted. The 3,000 flowering cherry trees were a gift from Japan and are still a major attraction for visitors and residents alike in the early days of spring.

For visitors to the city today, Washington falls naturally into half-a-dozen or so areas, each of which amply rewards several hours, or even days, spent exploring its sights and amenities. Old hands will advise the visitor to manage without a car in late spring and summer: Washington's monumental traffic jams are notorious, and there are other, less fraught ways of getting about. There is a modern rapid-transit rail Metro system

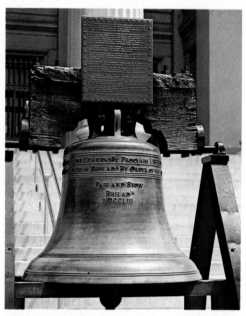

For air-travelers, their first glimpse of Washington is probably the futuristic Dulles International Airport below.
A reproduction of the famous Liberty Bell, above *commissioned by the Pennsylvania Provincial Assembly in 1751, is displayed in the National Archives Building, which also houses documents such as the Declaration of Independence and the Constitution. Although principally the home and office of the President of the United States, the White House* overleaf *is a museum of American history. The floodlit Capitol Building* right.

opened in 1976, special Tourmobile tram services, Metrobuses on all the main city streets, relatively inexpensive taxis, and, of course, the visitors' own feet, which can be the easiest way of getting about except in the height of Washington's humid and sun-drenched summer.

Departure point for most voyages of discovery around Washington is Capitol Hill, dominated by the U.S. Capitol Building itself, with the Supreme Court and Library of Congress buildings nearby. Also in this area are the Folger Shakespeare Library, with its replica of the Elizabethan theater, like Shakespeare's original Globe, and the U.S. Botanic Gardens.

The Mall is one of the major tourist attractions of Washington. It extends from the Capitol Building to the Lincoln Memorial, though the Mall area could be said to stretch to the Potomac River to include the Washington Monument and Jefferson Memorial and the Tidal Basin, where the beautiful cherry blossoms abound in the spring.

Along the Mall's tree-lined, grass-covered length are many of the city's important and most interesting buildings. The Voice of America studios are in the Health, Education and Welfare Building on Independence Avenue on the south

INTRODUCTION

worse by the fact that many streets were torn up while the Metro rail system was being built. The Metro has encouraged mass transit travel, and is helping to draw people back to the department stores along F and G Streets. There are a growing number of interesting restaurants and pubs in the area between Farragut Square and Dupont Circle, along with the many fun nightspots, bars and discotheques. A favorite tourist stop in downtown Washington is Ford's Theater, on 10th Street, where John Wilkes Booth shot Abraham Lincoln on that fateful night in April, 1865. This theater, where plays are once again performed regularly, has a museum of Lincoln relics in the basement. The Petersen House, where Lincoln was carried to die, is across the street.

The White House, official home of all U.S. presidents except George Washington, belongs to all Americans, literally, for it is

The National Visitor Center above, *with its magnificent arched ceiling, provides an information and orientation service for visitors to the capital. The "olde worlde" flavor has been retained at the Georgetown Tobacco Shoppe* right, *where pungent leaves of tobacco hang from the ceiling.*

side of the Mall; on Constitution Avenue, to the north, are the National Archives where the original Constitution, Bill of Rights and Declaration of Independence are on display; the Smithsonian Institution has several of its major buildings along the Mall, including the Museum of History and Technology, the Air and Space Building and the Natural History Building; the National Gallery of Art is on the corner of 6th and Constitution Avenue, the Federal Bureau of Investigation is in the new J. Edgar Hoover Building; and the Bureau of Engraving and Printing, where America's money is printed, is at 14th and C Streets.

From the Mall area, most people intent on discovering Washington will gravitate either north to the downtown area or northwest to the White House and Foggy Bottom.

Downtown Washington, the commercial and business center of the city, has had its ups and downs. For a time it went through a period of urban decay, made

INTRODUCTION

Restaurants in and around Washington offer a variety of cuisines, ensuring that the tourist will never go hungry! Shown above is Mr Henry's, on Wisconsin Avenue in Georgetown, while Julian serves the steaks in "Blackie's House of Beef" right, a popular tourist restaurant specializing, as the name suggests, in beef dishes.

kept up by public funds and most Americans feel that they have just as much right to walk through it as the President himself; hence the long lines of people waiting in East Executive Avenue five mornings a week, summer and winter, to get in to look through the few rooms open to the public. The White House is obviously the major attraction in this part of Washington, but also of interest are the U.S. Treasury, Blair House and St. John's Church.

The Department of State, George Washington University, the Watergate complex and the Kennedy Center lie to the west of the White House in an area of gracious old brick houses, smart new apartment blocks and tree lined streets stretching to the Potomac, which has taken on the unlikely nickname of "Foggy Bottom" – at first because of a gas works there, but since World War II as a sideswipe at the turgid, bureaucratic prose said to emanate from the State Department.

The northwest area of the city, north of the White House, is very much Diplomatic Washington, euphemistically known as "Embassy Row". Around the point where Massachusetts Avenue and 23rd Street intersect are the legations of many countries; there are more, especially

like in old Maryland before Washington city was ever imagined.

Not to be omitted from any survey of the interesting parts of Washington are three places which are outside the District of Columbia but are very much a part of the greater Washington area: Arlington, Alexandria and Mount Vernon.

Technically, Arlington County may be in the state of Virginia, but it is so closely linked with Washington – literally, by only a bridge, the Arlington Memorial Bridge, away from the Lincoln Memorial – as to seem part of the capital. The sense of being part of the capital is made even stronger by the looming presence of the massive Pentagon Building, office block of the nation's military might, just to the east. For most people, the name "Arlington" means not a county but a

of the newer African states, along 16th Street and Colorado Avenue, and others around the area reaching up to Rock Creek Park.

Probably of greater interest to the average visitor, who is unlikely to be invited to diplomatic cocktail parties anyway, will be delightful and elegant Georgetown, lying to the west, on the banks of the Potomac. Georgetown was once a thriving port and is now a very desirable residential area. Its tree lined streets are enlivened by good restaurants, art galleries and antique shops: perfect for strolling along and window-shopping, especially on balmy autumn days when the golds, reds and bronzes of the changing leaves seem so in keeping with the fine architecture of the houses. Georgetown University, with its twin spires prominent on the horizon, has been the training ground for many American diplomats. Some of the historic houses and gardens are open to the public, and give a glimpse of what life may have been

Based on a photograph of the historic moment when the American flag was raised on Mount Suribachi, after the storming of the beaches of Iwo Jima, this magnificent statue left, *by Felix De Waldron, symbolizes the courage and heroism of the Marine Corps.*

Overlooking the Potomac River, in tranquil and beautifully-landscaped hillsides, is the Arlington National Cemetery. Many of the Nation's greatest figures lie buried here, along with thousands of the men who died serving their country. Top left and right *are the graves of Senator Robert F. Kennedy and President John F. Kennedy, the latter being marked by an eternal flame. Above is the Tomb of the Unknown Soldiers, which contains the bodies of un-named soldiers who died during the Korean and both World Wars. The Tomb is continually guarded by members of the Old Guard.*

cemetery – the 420-acre National Cemetery, where many thousands of men who served in the nation's armed forces lie buried. Here, too, is the moving, simple grave of President John F. Kennedy, marked by an eternal flame; the grave of his brother Robert, and the Tomb of the Unknown Soldier.

A short walk from the Kennedy graves is Arlington House, built early in the nineteenth century by George Washington's foster son, George Washington Parke Custis, and for many years the home of the latter's daughter

The city is full of contrasts – from the colorful, exuberant cheerleaders at one of the Washington Bullets' home games left, *to the starkly beautiful East Building of the National Gallery of Art* right, *sharp and white against the brilliant blue sky.*

Mary and her husband, General Robert E. Lee. It is now restored and open to the public. The tomb of Pierre L'Enfant rests on the mansion's front lawns, and looks across the river to the great city L'Enfant planned.

Alexandria was originally a sister town to Georgetown, on the opposite bank of the Potomac, but where Georgetown has become just a suburb of Washington, Alexandria retains its own identity as a Virginia town dating from Colonial times. It even has many of the street names given it before George III was rejected as King of the American colonies: "King", "Prince", "Pitt" and "Royal", for instance, though "Lee" and "Union" Streets recall a later period of turmoil in the town's history. Old Town Alexandria, which contains many carefully preserved eighteenth-and nineteenth-century buildings, is of particular significance to anyone interested in pre-Independence history.

Nine miles south of Alexandria, and sixteen miles south of Washington, is Mount Vernon; George and Martha Washington's home. This beautiful, carefully preserved and restored mansion set in the well-kept grounds is a real jewel among Washington, D.C.'s attractions. The house itself is lovingly cared for, and in the grounds are a delightful flower garden, a spinning house, a coach house, the old slave quarters and other buildings which have been turned into a museum of eighteenth-century American life. The tomb of General Washington and his wife is also in the grounds, resting in the timeless peace and beauty of this lovely Virginia plantation.

It seems a long way in distance and time from the city Washington planned over 185 years ago. The United States' capital now is a great metropolis, thriving on a diet of politics, sometimes choked with traffic or consumed by the smog made from gasoline fumes, and always

alive to the voices of millions of people. Farmers from Kansas, oil millionaires from Texas, hippies from California, busloads of schoolchildren filling the Smithsonian's galleries, columns of protesters and marchers waving banners or sitting down in front of the White House, doctors, dentists, lawyers, car salesmen, parents and children, black and white from Our Town, USA – all come to Washington because it is the historic center and mainspring of the vast democracy George Washington may have hoped for but could hardly have believed possible in its twentieth-century reality.

A BRIEF HISTORY

Although Washington cannot trace its origins back to the earliest days of the American colonies and, indeed, was not thought of until the original thirteen colonies had become one nation, it is still a city steeped in history. It is not a long history – less than two hundred years – and in some ways it is rather inglorious. For much of the nineteenth century, Washington was a small town with more than its fair share of red light districts and dubious company, not enough accommodation and too many potholes in the street.

In other ways Washington has had a very glorious history because it has been the center from which a country that has become a world power has grown and reached out. It enshrines everything that has made the United States what it is today.

It was in 1790 that the U.S. Congress, having decided that the country must have a specially built federal capital, settled on 100 square miles of Maryland and Virginia as the site. In 1793, President George Washington laid the cornerstone of both the Capitol Building and the President's House, and in 1800 the two buildings were occupied.

In true democratic style, competitions had been held to find suitable designs for both buildings. The prize for the Capitol Building – $500, a gold medal and a piece of land in the new town – was won by a late entry from an amateur, Dr. William Thornton. James Hoban, designer of the President's House, was a professional architect, and a very good one. But amateur or professional, the two men set a style for the nation's capital which was to be copied by state capitals across the country.

Neither building was finished in 1800. President John Adams moved into his official residence from stylish Philadelphia to find himself without many of the amenities of civilized life, and Congress – 32 senators, 106 representatives, and a few dozen government clerks – found themselves a mile away over rough, swampy ground sharing the north wing of the Capitol Building with the Supreme Court and the Library of Congress.

It was all very makeshift and rather

like camping out. Those people lucky enough to find accommodation in Georgetown often could not get back to it if heavy rains made the roads impassable. Those not so fortunate found themselves in small cottages, shanties, or the one tavern Washington boasted. Many were the cries for abandoning this small village and returning to Philadelphia.

In one way, at least, the burning of the President's House and the Capitol Building by British troops in 1814 was a good thing: it stopped for the time being any thought of Congress's moving elsewhere, for nothing would look worse than a nation's government fleeing before its enemy.

So Congress stayed, the President's

The city's museums carry a wealth of absorbing displays and exhibits. The National Museum of History and Technology shows some of the world's greatest inventions like Bell's telephone, and Morse's telegraph. Above is a reconstruction of an early newspaper bureau, while left is the Prairie Schooner covered wagon. The Baldwin Locomotive is exhibited in the Arts and Industries Building below right. Above right is Ford's Theater with the Presidential box on the right, where Abraham Lincoln received the fatal bullet wound that ended his life.

House and the Capitol Building were rebuilt, and gradually Washington grew into a proper city. By 1840, when New York could count a population of 391,000 and New Orleans 102,000, Washington's population was still only 23,000. By 1860, it had grown to 61,000, and in the years following the Civil War, it grew rapidly, reaching well over 177,000 by 1880.

The Civil War was a difficult time for Washington. As a town, it was very much of the South, with its own slave markets, and slave ships moving up and down the Potomac River taking the slaves to the sugar and cotton plantations of the South. But as the capital of the United States, it was anti slavery and in Abraham Lincoln it

A BRIEF HISTORY

had a President dedicated to the abolition of this abominable practice.

No Civil War battle was ever fought in the streets of Washington, but the tide of battle came desperately close on several occasions, and the town became a vast training camp, hospital and mortuary, and a store for horses and cattle. In July 1861, the first Battle of Bull Run, in which the Union forces were defeated, was fought just 26 miles from Washington. Three years later, General Jubal Early led a band of Confederate raiders right to the outskirts of Washington before Union forces were able to drive them off.

One reason for the dramatic jump in Washington's population after the Civil War was the great influx of freed slaves, come to the capital in search of work and government protection. But there was not enough work for them all, and soon slums and hovels began to appear, especially in the southwest part of the city. Across the tracks, as it were, well-off whites, many of whom had closed up their Washington houses and left for Europe when the War began, were returning, and were soon followed by men with business interests intent on lobbying the government, and ready to spend any amount of money in doing so.

Washington was growing fast, and had definitely come to stay. After the 1870s, little more was heard of talk to move the government elsewhere. In 1871, the cornerstone was laid for what was to become, after seventeen years' construction, the world's biggest office block of its time, the State-War-Navy Building.

The Capitol Building right *is the decision-making center of the United States, where the U.S. Congress meets. One of its 540 rooms is the Statuary Hall* previous page, *refurbished to look as it did when the House met here between 1807 and 1857. Below is the memorial dedicated to the founder of the Smithsonian Institution, British scientist James Smithson.*

JAMES SMITHSON
FOUNDER OF THE SMITHSONIAN INSTITUTION
WHO DIED AT GENOA ITALY JUNE 26 1829
THESE HIS REMAINS WERE BROUGHT TO
THE UNITED STATES IN 1904 FOR REINTERMENT
IN THE CARE OF THE INSTITUTION HE FOUNDED

Clearly, Washington was beginning to think big.

The growth of the city continued, with most of Washington's development from a rather sleepy town into a major city taking place in the twentieth century. A new awareness of the importance of Washington's role as the representative of the whole nation in the eyes of the world, led to big efforts to beautify the city. Parks were planned and laid out, marshland taken over and converted into recreation areas, thousands of new houses built, and due attention was given to town planning in all its aspects.

Franklin Roosevelt's New Deal, with its emphasis on the creation of more and more federal agencies to help the U.S. out of the Depression of the 1930s, added to Washington's importance at the center of the nation's affairs. The city could at last

The most highly-prized documents housed in the National Archives building are the original Declaration of Independence, the Constitution and the Bill of Rights top right. More of the nation's treasures are contained in the Library of Congress, constructed in 1897. The Main Reading Room with its exquisite dome above was built in the Italian Renaissance style. Left is Petersen House, where Abraham Lincoln was taken after being shot at Ford's Theater.

be seen to have come of age: not necessarily the largest city in the U.S., but certainly the most important and influential.

The Marquis de Lafayette, America's first "honorary citizen", may have been a little carried away in his 1824 description of Washington, but today his words seem only right and proper: "The central star of the constellation which enlightens the whole world".

As Washington is the main body of government of the United States, so Capitol Hill is the heart. This is the place where the first stones were laid for the capital of the new nation, and it is still the point from which Washington measures its growth, both literally and figuratively.

Literally, the city is divided into quadrants according to lines drawn through Capitol Hill and its streets are

named in order east and west, north and south, of the Hill. Figuratively, the city draws its lifeblood from what happens on the Hill, and politics are very much the *raison d'être* of Washington; the speeches of Congressmen are discussed in bars and buses, the decisions of state are the staple diet of cocktail and dinner parties.

Left *is the façade of the Library of Congress, and* above *is the marble stairway leading to the Main Reading Room. The* Supreme Court above left and right *is reminiscent of a Greek Temple, and the panels on the heavy bronze doors trace the evolution of law from Ancient Greece to the present day.* Far left *is another view of the majestic Capitol Building.*

SEAT OF GOVERNMENT

Whatever else draws millions of people to Washington every year, it is the activities of the people on the Hill which arouse the greatest interest.

Dominating the Hill, with its nineteen-foot-tall statue of Armed Freedom on the Dome soaring 287 feet above the ground, is the Capitol Building itself, where the U.S. Congress meets. Although security is considerably tighter than it was, say, fifteen or twenty years ago, visitors are still welcome in the Capitol Building and see enough to get a good idea of how it works, whether or not Congress is in session.

Outside the building, on the East front steps, every President of the United States since Andrew Jackson has been inaugurated, each one taking an oath which has not changed since George Washington first spoke it in 1789. Great bronze doors show the way into a splendid building, nineteenth-century in style and decoration, which houses in one wing the Senate of the United States and, in the other, the House of Representatives.

The Capitol Building has an all-pervading sense of history about it, of momentous events and great political passions, which no visitor, whether American or foreign, can miss. He may even feel it under his feet as he stands on

the white circle in the middle of the floor of the rotunda, for here the bodies of military leaders, senators and Presidents, including Abraham Lincoln and John Kennedy, have lain in state. Above the rotunda soars the dome, with Constantino

The dome of the Capitol Building dominates the surrounding city left. Research facilities are also housed in the National Archives Building top. The Robert A. Taft Memorial above commemorates the man universally known as "Mr Republican". The tower contains a 27-bell carillon that chimes twice daily.

Brumidi's fresco of George Washington supported by Victory and Liberty, at its center. Brumidi spent years decorating the walls and ceilings of many of the rooms and corridors of the Senate Wing, covering them with a riot of vividly colored animals, birds, flowers and fruit. In recent years, the House of Representatives has undergone similar decorative treatment at the hands of Allyn Cox and his assistants, who have exchanged the democratically plain brown walls for scenes of life in the capital in the nineteenth century, and views of some of the state capitals.

The states of the U.S. are also represented in Statuary Hall, which was the meeting place of the House of Representatives until the mid-1850s. Now the Hall contains portrait statues of famous sons and daughters of the various states. Among other historic rooms in the Capitol Building open to visitors, is the ground floor room which once housed the U.S. Supreme Court and, before that, the Senate.

The magnificent lobby of the Supreme Court left *leads to the building's principal attraction, the courtroom* below, *considered the most impressive single public room in the United States.*

SEAT OF GOVERNMENT

The Supreme Court's present home stands opposite the East front of the Capitol Building, its marble walls and Corinthian-columned front dominated by the legend inscribed above it: "Equal Justice Under Law". The Supreme Court is more than simply the highest court in the land, for it is the court which interprets the Constitution – the very center of government and politics in the U.S. – and which therefore plays a major part in the decision-making process. Visitors can sit in on the court in session, though they may have to wait in line for a while, but it is well worth it.

Next door to the Supreme Court is another important part of the government decision-making process on Capitol Hill: the Library of Congress. This is one of the biggest libraries in the world and

The Library of Congress below, facing page left and previous pages is the largest library in the world, containing a superb collection of manuscripts, books, music, maps and prints. It also holds one of only three perfect copies of the Gutenberg Bible. The map and atlas department contains Pierre L'Enfant's original designs for Washington D.C.

library of its early days when it was set up around the nucleus of the 6,000 books from Thomas Jefferson's personal library.

Two thousand of Jefferson's books may still be found in the Rare Books Collection, which is just one of the many individual collections into which the Library is divided. Others include the Hispanic, Slav, Oriental, Law and Newspaper Libraries, the Archives of Folk Music, the Local History and Genealogy Room, the Manuscript Reading Room (which includes the papers of such diverse personalities as Sigmund Freud, Zane Grey, the Wright brothers of aviation fame, and Henry Kissinger), the Prints and Photographs Department, and the Film Collection.

Shown above and facing page, top *are two different views of the Capitol Building. Practically all the Presidents since Jackson have been inaugurated on the steps of this magnificent building.*

All these priceless collections are housed either in the splendid Classical-style main Library, with its circular main reading room, or in one of the Library extensions, the newest of which is the severely modern Madison Building.

These, then, are the major government buildings to be found in the Capitol Hill area. But perhaps to any ambitious member of the House of Representatives or any Senator ensconced in his office in the new Senate Building, which is connected to the Capitol Building by its own private subway, the most desirable building of all to be in is the one that is just a short Inauguration Day walk up Pennsylvania Avenue: the White House.

not to be missed by anyone interested in scholarship or really eager to know how Congress operates. The Library of Congress is a very finely equipped reference library indeed, and is used by scholars and students from all over the world although, as its name implies, its primary function is to provide information for Congress and government.

To this end, it takes in 7,000 new books each working day to add to the 18 million already there, has 117,000 periodicals in its files, newspapers from all over the world, a vast film and tape bank, and has set up Library of Congress centers in many cities of the world to ensure that important works published outside the U.S. and in languages other than English find their way back to the Library in Washington. Thus, the Library of Congress has become a major working tool of the U.S. Government, and a far cry from the select

THE YEAR'S ROUND

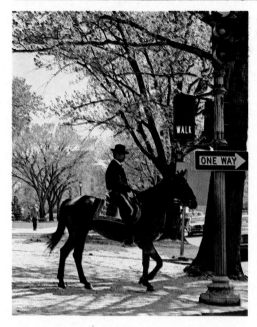

Washington, being the nation's capital, is, naturally, a city of parades, festivals and many colorful and moving annual events. Whether it be the Presidential inauguration; Easter egg rolling contest; Cherry Blossom Festival or Christmas tree-lighting ceremony–it is all part and parcel of an annual round of events as familiar as the opening of the new session of Congress each January or of the yearly term of the Supreme Court in October.

Washington is also a city on which the temperate nature of the climate imposes its own annual cycle of activity. Visit

Washington in the spring and you will find a city clothed in the delicate pastel colors of spring flowers, the pink of cherry blossoms and the tender green of young grass and new leaves. Come summertime the greens are harsher, more strident, and the air is heavy with humidity. By fall, the oak, elm and maple trees have blanketed the city with new and brilliant colors: the reds, yellows and oranges of the changing leaves fall from the trees to be scooped up from sidewalks and curbs by the men of the National Park Service. Winter is often white with snow, covering the trees along

The parks of Washington provide a welcome change of scenery for the weary tourist, and refreshment is provided by characters such as the lady above center with her bags of freshly-roasted peanuts. The other major feature of any city, of course, is its people, and Washington is fortunate in the richness and variety of life it contains.

Pennsylvania Avenue, where newly elected Presidents walk after their inauguration.

Washington's greatest festival and celebration bonanza happens only every four years, when the new president is inaugurated on January 20. From the East front steps of the Capitol Building the United States' new leader walks down the avenue to the White House, his home for the next four years. Despite television, which shows every detail of the great national event, the crowds are always thick along the parade route, and the rejoicing – even if the snow is knee-deep and the weather bitterly cold – is

Sport plays an important part in the average American's life. Basketball and ice-hockey are extremely popular, the local teams being the Washington Bullets and the Washington Capitals, respectively.

tremendous. The balls and receptions given by the victorious party fill the Washington night scene, in some contrast to the quiet which usually prevails over the city after dark, for Washington is not particularly noted as a city for night life.

If the Inauguration comes only every four years, there are other events that turn up annually in the President's diary, which are in their own way just as significant to the life of the country. At Easter, for instance, he will see his South Lawn invaded by children ready to roll brightly colored eggs down carefully marked lanes on the grass. This is an annual event which adults may attend only if they have a child as escort. But childless adults need not worry; they may well find an enterprising

young Washingtonian outside the White House perfectly willing to hire himself out for a few cents.

At Christmas the President switches on the lights of the National Christmas Tree and inaugurates a twelve-day Pageant of Peace.

Other important events in the President's diary are of a more solemn kind. On Memorial Day in May, he will lay a wreath on the Tomb of the Unknown Soldier at Arlington, paying homage to the nation's war dead. In November, Veterans Day honors those who have fought for their country, and in December the country remembers Pearl Harbor. Ceremonies are held each year at the Marines' Iwo Jima Memorial near Arlington National Cemetery.

For ordinary Washingtonians, every month of the year brings its events, parades, services and commemorations. In February, two great presidents, George Washington and Abraham Lincoln, are remembered on their birthdays. Lincoln's birthday, February 12, is not a public holiday, though Lincoln is honored in ceremonies at his Memorial. Washington's birthday is a public holiday, marked on the third Monday in the month, though it has become traditional for shops to stay open so that they can take part in city-wide sales where goods are marked down to unbelievably low prices.

March is the month for the Irish. This time it is Constitution Avenue's turn to see the big parade, a huge one in honor of St. Patrick on March 17, when Irish eyes are smiling and the air is full of song.

The end of March or beginning of April sees spring coming to Washington in a blaze of cherry blossom and for a week the Cherry Blossom Festival catches the whole city in its magic. There are balls, pageants, shows and concerts, pretty Cherry Blossom princesses and yet another parade to mark one of the most attractive times of year in Washington.

By June, the city is well out-of-doors. The two-day President's Cup Regatta takes place on the Potomac, and is the high point of the boating year. The Marine Parades, held on the Marine Barracks parade grounds in colorful military splendor on Friday evenings, will

have already begun and carry on to September. July and August see many outdoor events as part of the summer in the Parks program, while July 4 is a very special day, of course, marked by spectacle, bands and a grand fireworks' display near the Washington Monument.

The Festival of American Folklife, held under the auspices of the Smithsonian Institution, is fast becoming an annual

The Botanic Garden, featured on these pages, is housed in the greenhouse at the foot of Capitol Hill and contains an extensive permanent collection of tropical and subtropical plants. Its superb orchid collection is drawn from over 500 varieties and includes the brilliantly colored Cattleya Trianae far left center. Also among its exotic blooms are the Phar Edelweiss far left this page, the Paph Hailoa far left bottom, and the named varieties Barbara Billingsly (orange) and Margaret Stuart (white) shown far left top. Poinsettias above, along with many seasonal exhibits, can also be seen in this fascinating conservatory with its host of rare and unusual botanical specimens.

fixture for October. It usually takes place on the Mall, and visitors get an opportunity to become acquainted with the many aspects of American Folk art and culture.

Whatever the time of year, almost certainly there will always be more visitors and tourists than residents taking part in most of Washington's annual events. The city is most crowded during the pleasant three months of spring, from the end of March to June. In April alone something like five million people crowd into restaurants, hotels, and visit famous sights. It is just part of the price to be paid for being in one of the most popular cities in the United States.

THE WHITE HOUSE

The President of the United States lives at 1600 Pennsylvania Avenue, N.W. The pleasant, white-painted, neoclassical-style house in which he lives is set deceptively close to the road, easy to see over the railings, and cut off from passers-by only by lawns and trees. Apart from the laying-down of Pennsylvania Avenue, which was little more than a scratched-out track when the "President's House" was first occupied in 1800, this north view of the building has changed remarkably little in the years since the house was built.

President George Washington decided that the President of the United States must have an official residence, and it was he who selected the site – an orchard to the west of the site of the Capitol Building – and laid the cornerstone in October 1793. The building was based on a design by James Hoban, who had entered it in the competition which had been set up to find a fitting design for the building.

Washington died in 1799, before the house was completed, so the first President to live in the new official residence was John Adams. His wife, Abigail, who was

Set amid tranquil, landscaped gardens is the White House, the home of every President since John Adams.

also to see her son John Quincy Adams live in the White House as President, was a skilled social leader, setting a certain style of protocol around the Presidency. It is therefore ironic that the best-known legend to have come down from her time in the President's house was that she should have hung her washing to dry in the East Room. She had reason: the room was unfinished, and no-one had thought to provide her with a yard, or fences or

other conveniences. The lack of domestic conveniences was to be a constant cry of First Ladies at the White House in the years to come.

Since John Adams, thirty-seven presidents, their wives and families have lived in the Executive Mansion, the official name of the President's house from 1818 until Teddy Roosevelt made the unofficial "White House" official by using it on his letter head. There have been two major gaps in the occupancy of the White House. The first was for three years after British troops set fire to it in August 1814, apparently in retaliation for the burning of York (Toronto) by American soldiers during the 1812 – 14 War. Fortunately, a great thunderstorm put out the fire before the outer walls were destroyed, and after internal rebuilding, which turned out to have included a great deal of hasty covering up with white plaster and paint, plus a good coat of white paint on the outside to hide the smoke stains on the buff-coloured stone, the building was occupied again. It was this lavish use of white paint which led to the house being nicknamed "White House".

THE WHITE HOUSE

took their toll. So President Truman moved across the road to Blair House and an army of workers moved in, practically to rebuild the interior from scratch behind the shell of James Hoban's design.

Today, the White House stands as a major symbol of American life. It is the home of the First Family, where successive First Ladies have managed also to be wives and mothers; it is the Executive Office of the President, most of whose work is carried out not in the relatively small original house, but in the Executive Wings, one of which was added by Theodore Roosevelt and the other by Franklin Roosevelt; and it symbolizes the fact that the President embodies the nation as well as leads it. To Americans, as to the rest of the world, he is the voice of the nation, the man with whom the buck stops, as Harry Truman put it.

It is this symbolic role of the White House, as much as natural curiosity to see where the President lives, which brings thousands of people to wait outside the White House every morning from Tuesday to Saturday, to see inside the building. Unless they are lucky enough to get tickets for the special early-morning VIP tours, they do not, in fact, see a great deal.

The White House has 132 rooms, 54 of which are reserved exclusively for the private use of the First Family on the second and third floors. The visitors who line up in East Executive Avenue get to see just five, plus the entrance hall and corridors. But these five rooms on the first floor are the grand State Rooms of the White House and – apart from Lincoln's Room and the President's oval study on the second floor – are the most historic in the building.

The East Room is the White House's ballroom and grand reception room. Its simple classical lines are offset by white walls, rich window drapes and a brilliantly polished inlaid-wood floor. Three huge cut-glass chandeliers illuminate the scene, which may well be a concert, a play, or a Presidential press conference. Several weddings have taken place here, including that of Lyndon Johnson's daughter, Lynda. (President Nixon's daughter Tricia was married outside in the Rose Garden.)

The White House top *has undergone various modifications over the years, and bears the stamp of every President who has occupied it. Commanding a fine view of the north side of the White House is the equestrian statue of General Jackson.*

The second gap in occupancy came in 1948, when Harry Truman came back for his second term as President to find the huge East Room ceiling propped up by scaffolding, his own desk shaking on the floor of his study, and the whole building full of creaks and groans. Some people even said that the ghost of Lincoln still walked the corridors. The time had clearly come for the old building to be put right before years of damp foundations, propping up, patching and making do

The Green Room, Blue Room and Red Room make up a rich suite of rooms overlooking the South Lawn, each one leading into the other. The Green Room is a State sitting room, restored and furnished with eighteenth-century furniture and pieces brought in after the destructive 1814 fire.

The Blue Room is one of the famous oval rooms James Hoban included on the South front as innovations to his basically simple eighteenth-century gentleman's residence. The other oval room is the President's study on the floor above. The Blue Room has increasingly become a main entrance and reception room as more and more of the President's important guests arrive by helicopter on the South lawn, from which they walk up the steps to the South portico and so into the Blue Room.

The Red Room has been brilliantly decorated with fuschia-colored silk on the walls and Empire-style furniture. From there, the visitor passes into the State Dining Room, elegantly decorated in white and gold and dominated by a portrait of Abraham Lincoln in thoughtful pose. The room can seat well over a hundred guests, and many heads of state and other important people have dined here.

Unless they are lucky enough to catch a glimpse of him in a corridor or coming or going in a helicopter from the South Lawn, casual visitors to the White House are unlikely to see its famous occupant. There was a time when any citizen who cared to make the effort could visit the White House and shake hands with the President. But times have changed and security is much stricter. Even so, the words written by John Adams to his wife in the first letter he wrote from the White House, on November 2, 1800, are still apposite:

"I pray heaven to bestow the best of blessings on this house, and on all that shall hereafter inhabit it. May none but honest and wise men ever rule under this roof".

The sun sets behind the graceful Washington Monument right.

So you have visited Capitol Hill, inspected the Library of Congress, toured through the White House. What next? Well, plenty, for Washington is a city with much history behind it, and a lot happening right now, so there is more than enough to keep the visitor – and the resident – occupied.

For the visitor, a good place to put near the top of the list of things to see and do is the Washington Monument. A 555-foot-high stone obelisk, it is the tallest landmark in the city and a great place from which to get a bird's-eye view of how everything fits together. It stands in the center of the Mall area, between the White House and the Tidal Basin, and on a clear day offers splendid views over the city and into Maryland and Virginia. It is some time since anyone was allowed to walk up the 898 stairs to the viewing level – too many people could not make the climb and had to be rescued – so it is a ten-cent ride up in the elevator, though you can walk down if you prefer.

The Washington Monument seen from various angles: from Arlington National Cemetery left, *reflected in the waters of the Tidal Basin* top right, *towering over the White House* above, *and from one of Washington's many beautiful parks* center right. *Built to commemorate two more American Presidents, the Lincoln Memorial* bottom right *is sited at the end of the Mall, while the beautiful Jefferson Memorial overleaf stands on the south bank of the Tidal Basin.*

SIGHTS TO SEE

From the Washington Monument, a short walk leads to the Lincoln Memorial at the west end of the Mall area on the banks of the Potomac; a beautiful site for a moving and lovely shrine, built in the calmly serene style of a classic Greek temple. The superbly carved marble figure of the murdered president gazes toward the Washington Monument across a limpid pool of water. All now is peace and serenity after the drama of the Civil War and the horror of the shooting in Ford's Theater. This is a place where Americans can reaffirm their belief in their nation, and many do just that by murmuring the well-remembered words of two of Lincoln's most famous speeches, the Second Inaugural Address and the Gettysburg Address, which are carved in stone inside the Memorial.

The Jefferson Memorial is also built of white marble, in domed classical style, and is on the southern side of the Tidal Basin. It has a bronze statue of Thomas Jefferson, Declaration of Independence in hand, at

The majestic statue of Abraham Lincoln above and right *dominates the Lincoln Memorial* below. *Lincoln, the 16th President, is shown as a stern but just man, beset by the problems of what was a difficult period in American history.*

its center and some of his famous writings carved on the wall, including "I have sworn upon the altar of God eternal hostility against every form of tyranny over the mind of man…"

The Lincoln and Jefferson memorials are both places to stand and quietly contemplate the enormous achievements of America in its relatively short existence. Another is the Smithsonian Institution, a series of places where the multitudinous achievements of all mankind can be marveled at.

The Smithsonian Institution was begun on a legacy of a few boxfuls of gold coins from an Englishman, James Smithson. The original Smithsonian was in a small building on the Mall, which still houses administrative offices and a visitors' information center. The Institution itself has now spread over much of Washington and even into New York and Boston, as well as outside the United States, perpetuating James Smithson's aim, "the increase and diffusion of knowledge among men".

Among its dozen component parts in Washington are the National Museum of History and Technology, which gathers together many fascinating aspects of

IN THIS TEMPLE
AS IN THE HEARTS OF THE PEOPLE
FOR WHOM HE SAVED THE UNION
THE MEMORY OF ABRAHAM LINCOLN
IS ENSHRINED FOREVER

SIGHTS TO SEE

American life and history; the National Air and Space Museum, a superb modern complex with a stunning exhibition covering every facet of aviation and space exploration; the National Gallery of Art, one of the finest art collections in the country, counting superb works by Rembrandt, da Vinci, Vermeer, Goya, the Impressionists and twentieth-century artists in its coverage of six centuries of Western European and American art; and the Hirshhorn Museum, which concentrates on twentieth-century painting and sculpture. All these Smithsonian museums and collections are along the Mall, where several other Smithsonian galleries and collections may be found, which must make Washington's Mall one of the most rewarding and visually exciting cultural thoroughfares in the world.

For Americans who want to know more about their own past, rather than that of their nation, the place to go is the National Archives Building, in downtown Washington in the Federal Triangle. It is here that some very important relics of the nation's history are housed, including the original Declaration of Independence and the Constitution of the United States with its Bill of Rights. But it is also a

Throughout the National Air and Space Museum's twenty-four galleries are the aircraft, rockets and missiles that reveal man's airborne achievements. Among the many exciting exhibits are the Apollo Lunar Landing Module bottom left, *the docking Apollo and Soyuz rockets* far right top, *the Lunar Rover* far right center *and the Rocket Room* below. *Theaters, slide-shows, diagrams and dioramas, and a unique Spacearium are*

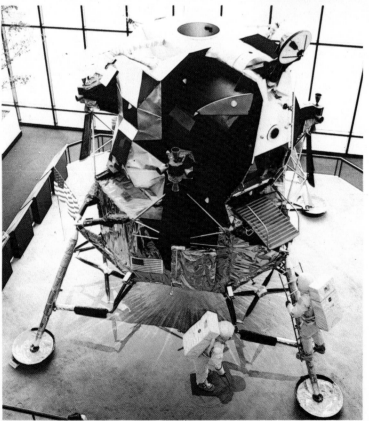

additional attractions in this fascinating Museum, part of the Smithsonian Institution, which, with its large library and research facilities make it one of the world's outstanding centers for historical aerospace research.

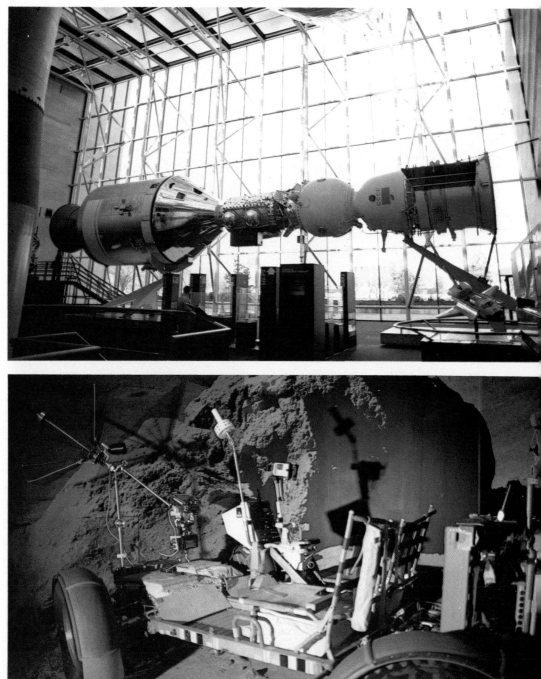

repository for a huge collection of federal records and documents, and is constantly used by scholars, historians and researchers, as well as by genealogists and the many ordinary people spurred into looking up their past by the phenomenal success of Alex Haley's book and television series, "*Roots*".

Television has no doubt influenced watchers to visit the Federal Bureau of Investigation, too, for in the J. Edgar Hoover FBI Building in the Federal

Triangle area, visitors can be taken on a tour that is like a background seminar on all those detectives and police series. You can see how the police laboratories use science to track down criminals, study photographs of the nation's Ten Most Wanted Fugitives, and watch a display of an FBI agent's chilling accuracy with a gun, which would surely scare anyone off the idea of trying a TV-style shoot-out with such a formidable opponent.

The FBI Building is always a sure-fire

SIGHTS TO SEE

Four of the treasures housed in the National Gallery of Art are: Renoir's "Girl with a Watering Can" below, Picasso's "The Lovers" below right, a self-portrait of Rembrandt facing page left, and Gainsborough's portrait of the Honourable Mrs Graham right.

hit with children; conversely the Bureau of Engraving and Printing, south of the Mall on 14th Street, is of keen interest to their parents, for it is here that America's paper money is printed, along with its postage stamps, passports and other important papers. Visitors may see the whole printing process, no doubt slightly stunned by the sight of all those stacks of dollar bills sitting there. The Bureau prints approximately 12 million notes a day, with one-dollar bills making up the major part of the printing.

Although the sights just described are generally considered the most important in Washington, there are still very many more well worth seeing, and varied enough to cater to all tastes and interests. There is the Folger Shakespeare Library, for instance, with its re-creation of an Elizabethan theater, or the nineteenth-century Ford's Theater and Lincoln Museum. For history buffs, there are the National Historical Wax Museum with its tableaux of high points in U.S. history, National Geographic's Explorers' Hall, or the Museum of the Daughters of the American Revolution. Or one could try the U.S. Botanical Gardens in its huge greenhouse near Capitol Hill, the Museum of African Art or the Corcoran Gallery of Art. Washington has something for everyone.

The Sculpture Garden, adjacent to the Hirshhorn Museum, contains a rectangular reflecting pool and around 75 pieces of sculpture, including the shimmering sphere below and Alexander Calder's "Two Discs" right. The Museum houses a magnificent collection of 20th century paintings and sculpture.

Below is the superb rotunda of the National Gallery of Art, while overleaf stands the 19-foot figure of Thomas Jefferson.

WE HOLD THESE TRUTHS TO BE SELF-
EVIDENT: THAT ALL MEN ARE CREATED
EQUAL, THAT THEY ARE ENDOWED BY THEIR
CREATOR WITH CERTAIN INALIENABLE
RIGHTS, AMONG THESE ARE LIFE, LIBERTY
ND THE PURSUIT OF HAPPINESS, THAT
SECURE THESE RIGHTS GOVERNMENTS
ARE INSTITUTED AMONG MEN. WE···
SOLEMNLY PUBLISH AND DECLARE, THAT
THESE COLONIES ARE AND OF RIGHT
OUGHT TO BE FREE AND INDEPENDENT
STATES···AND FOR THE SUPPORT OF THIS
DECLARATION, WITH A FIRM RELIANCE
ON THE PROTECTION OF DIVINE
PROVIDENCE, WE MUTUALLY PLEDGE
OUR LIVES, OUR FORTUNES AND OUR
SACRED HONOUR.
THOMAS JEFFERSON
1743–1826

EXPLORING THE ENVIRONS

Washington the city is comparatively small, but Washington the metropolis spread far into the surrounding states of Maryland and Virginia, and major highways, Metroliner trains, and assorted air services bring many other towns and cities well into the capital's orbit.

Many Washington workers do not live within the D.C. boundaries but in such attractive and often expensive areas as Chevy Chase, Maryland, or the custom-designed suburb of Reston, Virginia, 18 miles west of Washington. Here, Robert Simon hoped to create a self-contained community but he ran out of money and

had to sell to the mighty Gulf Oil Corporation, which has turned Reston into a well-heeled commuter paradise.

Whether they live in attractive suburbs or the crowded city, most Washingtonians occasionally feel like getting away from it all. It's partly the hurly-burly and non stop drama of life in politics, be they national or international, and partly the overwhelming humidity of the Washington summer, that drives people out. They are lucky in that they have plenty of places to which they can escape.

Near at hand, the lucky Washingtonian may have a horse or two stabled somewhere over the D.C. line in Maryland or Virginia so that he may play polo or hunt regularly. There are several hunts in the beautiful Virginia countryside, not always catching foxes, but retaining the traditions – pink coats and all – of a sport which George Washington loved.

Also not too far away, the Washingtonian may have been lucky enough to secure a berth for his boat in the harbor at Alexandria or, eastward into Maryland, at Annapolis.

The town and resorts of the Atlantic coast are only a few hours away by car, and a drive to the coast is the reason that many city workers give for leaving their offices early on a Friday. They want to avoid the great traffic jams which all too often build up near the Chesapeake Bay bridge at Annapolis, but their hopes are often unrealized, so they take the traffic snarls in their stride.

Annapolis, the capital of Maryland since 1694, is just a short drive along Route 50 from Washington, and has become a popular weekend retreat for well-to-do people from the city, many of

John F. Kennedy was involved in the restoration of Lafayette Square below right, *on the north-west side of which can be seen the Church of Presidents* above right. *Georgetown boasts some of the loveliest restored houses in America, one of which is the Marbury-Kennedy House* center left, *famous as the residence of President Kennedy. The oldest surviving building is the Old Stone House below left.*

whom keep second homes and luxury-style boats there, as well as a popular calling place for tourists in the area. Home of the U.S. Naval Academy, center of a lively fishing industry and of a rich sailing and boat-building community, Annapolis sits elegantly on the shore of Chesapeake Bay, with the sea breezes adding a pleasant tang to the attractive, Colonial-style eighteenth-century buildings along the waterfront. There's also an interesting mixture of people to add to the atmosphere: fishermen, perhaps with fresh catches of crabs and oysters, amateur sailors in the casual stylishness of jeans and sneakers, and state politicians and businessmen.

Its rich colonial past draws many visitors to Annapolis each year. This was the town where General Washington, in a tearful scene, resigned his command of the army, and where the peace treaty with Britain was ratified after the American Revolution. Both events took place in the State House, which is still in use today. The U.S. Naval Academy enshrines 300 years of naval history and tradition in its museum, and welcomes aboard over a million visitors a year. They come to take in the atmosphere of brisk naval spit and polish, to see John Paul Jones' burial place in the crypt of the Academy's chapel, and to watch the dress parades at Worden Field.

A drive west and south of Washington into Virginia can also lead back into the heart of pre-Revolutionary America, to a string of places associated with high points in American history from the

Mount Vernon right *was for many years the home of the Washington family and George Washington* above *is said to have spent his happiest days here.* Below *is the attic bedroom of the Old Stone House in Georgetown.*

earliest settlements through the days of the Revolution and the drama of the Civil War. Alexandria, Fredericksburg, Charlottesville, Richmond, Williamsburg, Jamestown, Yorktown were all towns of the Old Dominion of Virginia, the oldest settled in America, when Washington was still part orchard and part swamp. To visit these towns and such plantations as Mount Vernon, Ashlawn and Monticello – as many thousands of Washingtonians and visitors to Washington do each year – is to get caught up in the atmosphere of the eighteenth-century world of a proud, independent people who would defy a king and his army rather than pay an unfair tax.

The Colonial atmosphere is at its strongest in Williamsburg, once the capital of Virginia and now possessing in that part of town known as Colonial Williamsburg a carefully, lovingly restored evocation of eighteenth-century life in America. Today horses and carriages trot down its streets carrying people in jeans and sweat shirts with cameras in their hands, rather than men and women in the more elaborate dress of two hundred years ago, but the buildings they pass still appear as they were when they were first built, and Colonial Williamsburg has become a living, working museum of American life before the Revolution. Huge injections of Rockefeller money have made it all possible. It was John D. Rockefeller, Jr. who began taking an interest in Williamsburg in the 1920s, and the Rockefeller estate still funds the work there.

Although Richmond, which took over from Williamsburg as capital of Virginia in 1780, is also an old town, it contains more relics of the Civil War period than any other, for this was Robert E. Lee's town, a fact which the visitor is not allowed to forget. Lee's house on Franklin Street is one of the city's important shrines, and there is a Museum of the Confederacy and the Richmond National Battlefield Park to be seen as well. There are reminders of earlier days, of course, most notably the very beautiful Capitol Building, which Virginians consider the most beautiful in the United States, and which was designed by

Thomas Jefferson. Even the huge Philip Morris cigarette factory on the outskirts of town reminds one of the past, for many of the rich plantation owners of the eighteenth century made their fortunes from growing tobacco.

Thomas Jefferson's name prevails in this part of Virginia, as it does in Washington, for the lovely Monticello plantation was his, the University of Virginia at Charlottesville was founded and its buildings designed by him, and he

The stunning Mormon Tabernacle left is situated in Kensington, Maryland. Exhibits such as models of the late Jurassic dinosaurs top and the 92-foot model of a blue whale are on display at the National Museum of Natural History, where the collection exceeds 60 million objects.

designed and built Ashlawn, President James Monroe's home, also near Charlottesville.

Washington is one of the fastest-growing metropolitan areas in the U.S. Its population long ago spilled over the confines of the District of Columbia into the surrounding counties of Virginia and Maryland. The metropolitan area now has a population of nearly three million. In the inner urban area of D.C., the majority of the population is black; there are problems of unemployment and poor housing, despite strenuous efforts at redevelopment.

For Washingtonians of the District of Columbia, there is another big cause of discontent – and a surprising one in the capital of a nation which once went to war on a slogan of "no taxation without representation": the people of Washington cannot vote for their own senators or representatives in Congress. Washington is not a state or part of one, but an area of land ceded to the federal government, and its laws, even down to such minor matters as the flying of kites in Washington's parks or the sweeping up of leaves in autumn,

Reflected in the waters of the Potomac River is the John F. Kennedy Center, Washington's leading showpiece for the performing arts above. Its superb Opera House is shown facing page top. Below is the FBI Building, named after its long-term director.

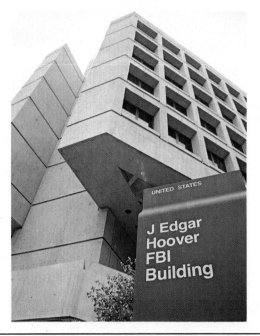

have been matters for Congress. Since 1973, when Congress approved a bill for home rule of a sort, voters have been able to choose their own mayor and council, but Congress still has the final say over municipal spending and has the power of veto.

Despite the fact that it "takes an Act of Congress" – a phrase which suggests to a Washingtonian vast areas of bureaucratic slowness and delay – to achieve anything in Washington, the city is on the whole an interesting and exciting place in which to live and work, with much of its beauty due to careful planning by caring people.

The city has a relatively high percentage of its total land area devoted to parks and recreation grounds, and organizations like the National Park Service ensure that they are carefully maintained so that joggers, walkers, cyclists, hikers, horse riders, picnickers, or simply carriage pushing parents can share and enjoy park amenities to the full.

The large and beautiful Rock Creek

tourists rather than grain, flour, coal or wood. The canal's towpath is a favorite track with cyclists and walkers, and its banks are used by fishermen and picnickers.

Twelve miles up the canal from Georgetown is Great Falls Park, probably the most beautiful park in metropolitan Washington, apart from Rock Creek. The Park is split in two by the Potomac River, with some of the best views of the 76-foot-high waterfalls to be had from the Virginia side.

For Washingtonians who want to feed the mind as well as exercise the body, the city has a strongly based cultural life.

Explorers Hall, contained within the offices of the National Geographic Society, displays the world's largest free-moving globe below left and below, *with a circumference of 34 feet. Overleaf is the interior of Washington National Cathedral.*

Park, like Potomac Park near the Tidal Basin, was planned in the 1890s. Rock Creek Park, where Teddy Roosevelt used to go riding, covers over 1,600 acres in the north-west quadrant and is still very much the beautiful, forested valley it was before it was turned into a National Park. Within its confines are picnic groves, an old flour mill, Pierce Mill, restored and operating again, a Nature Center which aims to foster a greater understanding and knowledge of outdoor life, and the National

Zoological Park, founded in 1889 and home, among hundreds of other birds and animals, to rare Bengal tigers and a pair of giant pandas.

The Chesapeake and Ohio Canal, which runs from Georgetown to Maryland, is another interesting part of outdoor Washington. The canal was a commercial waterway in the nineteenth century, but today the mule-drawn barges carry

There is always plenty of music, drama and other activities going on – some of it even performed free of charge.

Top cultural attraction in Washington, partly just because it is so big, must be the John F. Kennedy Center for the Performing Arts, on New Hampshire Avenue, NW. The Center does put on a large number of free events, including lectures, symposiums and the like, but it is also the

preserves and shows all kinds of movies from the earliest days of film-making in the United States to the present.

Some of the best music-making in Washington can be found outside regular concert halls. The Library of Congress provides a winter season of concerts so good (and usually performed by the world's best musicians sometimes even using the Library's precious collection of historic instruments) that there is always a scramble for tickets. The National Gallery of Art has its own orchestra and also sponsors concerts by visiting artists, often given among the trees and fountains of one of its garden courts. The bands of the Armed Forces can be found giving outdoor concerts all over Washington in the summer, in places like the West Terrace of the Capitol Building, the Jefferson Memorial, the Washington Monument or out at Arlington by the Iwo Jima Marine War Memorial.

Washington has plenty to offer theater buffs too. Foremost among the professionals is the Arena Stage, internationally recognized as a major producer of American drama. The National Theater, which dates back to the 1830s, is among the oldest in America, while one consistently excellent center of drama in the capital is to be found at Catholic University, which has a flourishing drama department and its own theater, the Hartke.

Being the national capital, Washington has a wide-ranging collection of excellent libraries, museums and art galleries to its credit, some of which, like the Library of Congress and the Smithsonian Institution, are known to scholars the world over, and all of which give Washingtonians and visitors free access to what is among the most varied collections of top quality specialist museums and galleries in the U.S.

Architecturally, Washington has grown into a quiet, rather than a strident twentieth-century city. This is partly because building regulations do not usually permit buildings to exceed in height the width of the street on which they stand. There have been exceptions, but nothing has been allowed to grow so

Washington caters for most religious denominations. The exquisite interior of the Islamic Center is shown above, *a beautiful mosque which is the center of Muslim worship and learning in America. Maintained by the Order of Friars Minor, the Byzantine Franciscan Monastery contains many replicas of Holy Land sites* top.

place for grand nights, evening dress and expensive seats, especially in the Opera House, where the great ballet and opera companies of America and Europe perform regularly. The Center's Concert Hall is now the home of the National Symphony Orchestra, the Eisenhower Theater is an important place for drama, and the American Film Institute Theater

For the visitor to Washington, the most striking impression of the city must be the myriad beautiful buildings lining spacious streets and attractive squares. Shown here are: the Executive Office Building below, a baroque structure including 900 Doric columns; the U.S. Treasury Department center right, considered to be one of the finest examples of Greek Revival architecture in America; the 17th Street Building bottom left, and the Washington National Cathedral bottom right. Spencer Fullerton Baird, second Secretary of the Smithsonian Institution, is commemorated by the Monument, top right.

high that it dominates the Capitol Building or the Washington Monument.

If rather too much public office building since the 1930s has been accomplished in a slightly heavy style, left to stand in acres of parking lots, there has still been much of interest and elegance achieved as well, including several religious buildings. The foundation stone of Washington's National Cathedral was laid in 1907 and the building, which is in the Gothic style and makes use of fine stained glass and carving, is not expected to be finished until the mid-1980s. St. Sophia's Greek Orthodox Church has a mosaic-covered interior which is a striking reminder of the Middle East rather than America, as is the Islamic Mosque, whose minaret can be seen over the trees of Rock Creek Park. They have been appropriate additions to a city which is as much of the world as it is of America.

First English edition published in 1981 by Colour Library International Ltd.
This edition is published by Crescent Books, Distributed by Crown Publishers Inc.
Illustrations and text © : Colour Library International Ltd. 163 East 64th Street, New York 10021.
Colour separations by FERCROM, Barcelona, Spain.
Display and text filmsetting by Focus Photoset, London, England.
Printed by Cayfosa and bound by Eurobinder - Barcelona (Spain)
All rights reserved.
Library of Congress Catalog Card Number: 81-67579
CRESCENT 1981